JAMES
MEREDITH

and School
Desegregation

by Dan Elish

GATEWAY CIVIL RIGHTS
THE MILLBROOK PRESS
BROOKFIELD, CONNECTICUT

Photographs courtesy of Mississippi Division of Tourism:
cover; UPI/Bettmann Newsphotos: pp. 1, 14, 20, 22;
Charles Moore, Black Star: pp. 2–3, 24; © Flip Schulke:
pp. 4, 18, 19, 26; The Schomburg Center, New York
Public Library: pp. 7 (both), 8 (both); AP/Wide World
Photos: cover inset, pp. 11, 17, 27, 29, 30.

Published by The Millbrook Press
2 Old New Milford Road, Brookfield, Connecticut 06804

Library of Congress Cataloging-in-Publication Data
Elish, Dan.
James Meredith and school desegregation / Dan Elish.
p.   cm.—(Gateway civil rights)
Includes bibliographical references and index
Summary: Focuses on the events surrounding James
Meredith's efforts to be allowed to attend the University
of Mississippi in 1962.
ISBN 1-56294-379-0 (lib. bdg.) ISBN 1-56294-861-X (pbk.)
1. Afro-Americans—Civil rights—Mississippi—Juvenile
literature. 2. Meredith, James—Juvenile literature.
3. University of Mississippi—Juvenile literature. 4.
College integration—Mississippi—Juvenile literature.
5. Mississippi—Race relations—Juvenile literature. [1.
Meredith, James. 2. Afro-American—Biography. 3.
Afro-Americans—Education. 4. School   integration.
5. Mississippi—Race relations.] I. Title. II. Series.
E185.93.M6E43   1994
323.1′196073—dc20   93-9383 CIP AC

Federal marshals rolled into town to keep the peace when Meredith tried to enroll at the Oxford campus of the University of Mississippi.

On *September 30, 1962*, President John F. Kennedy went on television and spoke to the students of the University of Mississippi. "The eyes of the nation and all the world are upon you," he said, "and upon all of us." For the first time in the history of the United States, a young black man was trying to enroll in that all-white school. His name was James Meredith.

Protesters had come out in full force on the university campus in the southern town of Oxford. By the time Kennedy gave his speech, rioting had begun. Federal marshals were called in to keep the peace. They used tear gas in an attempt to calm the angry crowd.

The fight raged through the night. "This is the worst thing I've seen in forty-five years," said President Kennedy with great sadness.

How had this come to pass? Why did America, "home of the free," need to call in troops to enroll a lone African American in a public university?

In the early sixties, the South remained a highly segregated part of the country. Whites lived separately from blacks. They were usually better off, and they went to their own schools.

On September 30, 1962, tear gas canisters
exploded on the Ole Miss campus as marshals
tried to keep rioters under control.

Many white Southerners, comfortable with their way of life, were ready to fight to keep things that way. It took the courage of such people as James Meredith to break down these racial barriers and start the South—and the nation—down the road to fairness.

"Separate But Equal"

James Howard Meredith was born on June 25, 1933, in Kosciusko, Mississippi, in the fertile lowlands east of the Mississippi River. His father was a successful farmer. James was a quiet boy, a bit of a loner. He studied hard at school, and his father was impressed by the amount of reading he did on his own.

It was clear from an early age that James was brave, too. He did not scare easily. He felt no fear walking alone through the woods near his house at night.

At the age of fifteen, James was a student at Kosciusko's Tipton High School. One day he was riding a train and was told to move to the black section. Even though this was common practice in the South, he cried angrily all the way home.

James grew up in a state whose flag was a copy of the one used by the Confederates during the Civil War. The South had lost its battle to keep slaves and separate from the rest of the

country. The Civil War, fought between 1861 and 1865, was long over, and the blacks of Mississippi had been free for generations. But their freedom was limited by racist attitudes that did not go away.

Blacks lived in a segregated world, where an invisible color line separated them from whites. So-called Jim Crow laws kept them down. These laws dictated acceptable behavior in public. Black people were not allowed to use bathrooms and drinking fountains marked "whites only." They were barred from restaurants and hotels. They sat in the back of buses and trains, and even shopped at separate stores. If a black man committed a crime, especially against a white person, he was often severely punished. If a white man committed a crime against a black man, he would most likely go free.

Signs told blacks where they could and could not go throughout the South.

James was very sensitive to racial issues. He was particularly upset by the gross unfairness of the Mississippi school system. In 1896 the Supreme Court had ruled that it was legal for schools to remain "separate but equal." In other words, whites did not have to attend the same schools as blacks, as long as the black schools were of good quality. However, this was not the case.

During 1950 the state of Mississippi spent $78.70 for each white student and only $23.83 for each black student. White classes were smaller and the instruction was much better. Teachers in white schools were paid twice as much money.

Not until 1954 would the U.S. Supreme Court rule
that segregated schools were unconstitutional. Here
is a typical rural black classroom and a white one.

Black school buildings were in terrible shape. Many black schools did not even have desks, and books were scarce.

James was frustrated by the poor education he received in his all-black school. So, at age seventeen, he moved in with his uncle in St. Petersburg, Florida. He had been one of the smartest students in his class in Mississippi. At his new school in Florida, he had to struggle to keep up. He saw clearly what a difference a good education made.

For years, James had dreamed of going to the University of Mississippi, one of the best colleges in his state. But he knew that "separate but equal" laws would keep him in a lesser quality, all-black school. Discouraged, he decided to join the military. On July 28, 1951, he volunteered for the Air Force and put his dream of a good and fair education on hold.

Coming Home

Meredith did well in the military. He rose to the rank of staff sergeant. He met and married his wife and had a son. But all the time he served his country, he planned to return to Mississippi and go to college.

It was 1960 before Meredith made it home. While he was in the service, the landmark Supreme Court decision of 1954, *Brown* v. *Board of Education of Topeka,* had struck down the doctrine of "separate but equal." It was now federal law that every school be integrated, or open to all races. Some people were overjoyed. Many Southerners, though, refused to obey the new law. Racism did not simply fade away because a law was passed.

This did not stop Meredith. He decided to start by taking some courses at all-black Jackson State College. He hoped that these would prepare him for the University of Mississippi, better known as Ole Miss.

Meredith could have gone to a racially mixed school in the North if he had wanted to. Why was he set on going to the University of Mississippi? The answer lay in his long-held dreams. From the time he was in high school, his goals had not changed. "I want to be a man," he said, "run for governor of the state of Mississippi, and get a degree from the University of Mississippi."

Meredith never really wanted to be governor. But, as he later wrote, "I simply wanted to run and get the vote of every Negro in Mississippi." Ole Miss was one of the most respected schools in the state. Anyone who wanted to amount to something simply had to go there. So far, not one black student had ever done so.

A year later, after a good deal of thought, Meredith decided it was time to act. The first thing he did was visit Medgar

Evers, the local field secretary of the powerful civil rights group the National Association for the Advancement of Colored People (NAACP). Evers instantly offered NAACP legal support to Meredith. With the words of John F. Kennedy's inaugural address ringing in his ears—"Ask not what your country can do for you; ask what you can do for your country"—Meredith dashed off a note to the registrar of the University of Mississippi asking for an application form.

Medgar Evers (right), field secretary of the NAACP, supported Meredith's efforts to enroll at Ole Miss. Evers was killed in front of his home in 1963.

When he received the form, he found that he needed to list five university graduates as character references. This was a problem. Meredith did not know any alumni. Besides, no white graduate would want to help him out. Meredith told Medgar Evers about the requirement. The two men decided that he should give the names of five responsible black Mississippians instead.

A few days later, Meredith mailed his application. The last thing he did before he sealed the envelope was to staple a photograph of himself onto the form.

"All the News That's Fit to Print"

The New York Times.

LATE CITY EDITION
Fair and cool today. Mostly sunny, continued cool tomorrow.

Temperature Range Today—Max., 60; Min., 53
Temperature Yesterday—Max., 69; Min., 64
Full U.S. Weather Bureau Report, Page 31

VOL. CIII...No. 35,178.

Entered as Second-Class Matter, Post Office, New York, N.Y.

NEW YORK, TUESDAY, MAY 18, 1954.

Copyright, 1954, by The New York Times Company.

Three Cents New York City, N. Y."
Elsewhere Accordingly.

FIVE CENTS

HIGH COURT BANS SCHOOL SEGREGATION; 9-TO-0 DECISION GRANTS TIME TO COMPLY

BROWN v. BOARD OF EDUCATION

In 1950 an African American, Oliver Brown, decided to do something about his daughter's education. The Browns lived in Topeka, Kansas, five blocks away from an all-white elementary school. Because the school was segregated, Brown had to take his daughter, Linda, across the railroad yard to a bus that took her twenty blocks away to an all-black school.

Brown and a dozen other black parents sued the city of Topeka to end the segregated school system. They said that the policy of ''separate but equal'' violated their rights as guaranteed in the Fourteenth Amendment of the Constitution.

It took until 1954 for the case, *Brown* v. *Board of Education of Topeka,* to reach the Supreme Court. Arguing for Brown was a distinguished black lawyer, Thurgood Marshall. Representing the state of Kansas were some of the best legal minds in the South.

On Monday, May 17, 1954, Chief Justice Earl Warren announced the Court's unanimous decision. ''In approaching this problem,'' he said, ''we cannot turn the clock back. . . . We must consider public education in the light of its full development and its present place in American life throughout the nation. . . . We conclude that in the field of public education the doctrine of 'separate but equal' has no place. Separate educational facilities are . . . unequal.''

The Decision
of the Court

Over the next two years, the university and the Mississippi state government and courts did everything they could to keep James Meredith out of Ole Miss. The man in charge of admitting students, Registrar Robert Ellis, began stalling right away. First, he told Meredith that he had applied too late. Then the University Board of Trustees tightened the rules for students who were transferring from other schools.

Meredith wrote a letter to Thurgood Marshall, the chief lawyer for the NAACP (and future Supreme Court justice), asking for more help. Marshall wrote back that he was "vitally interested" and turned Meredith's case over to a young black attorney, Constance Baker Motley.

Motley began by writing many unanswered letters to the university. Finally she wrote to the dean of the college. She spelled out her belief that Meredith was being turned down because of his race.

A week later, the university changed its policy yet again. This time it said that the courses Meredith had taken at Jackson State did not meet its standards.

Motley decided that it was time to go to court. A hearing was set for June 12, 1961. Midway through the opening of the court session, Federal District Judge Sidney C. Mize mysteri-

James Meredith with his lawyers, Constance Motley and Jack Greenberg.

ously put off the hearing until July 10. This delay caused Meredith to miss the university's first summer session. Then Judge Mize put the hearing off again until August 10, claiming that there was a conflict on his calendar. Because of this delay, Meredith missed the second summer session, too.

When the third court date finally came, Registrar Ellis took the stand and defended the university's policies. He said he was "shocked" that Meredith accused the university of denying him entrance based on his race. Ellis went on to say that Meredith had been rejected for many other reasons. Jackson State was not a good enough school from which to transfer. Meredith's letters of reference were not from Ole Miss alumni. Ellis even suggested that Meredith was a "bad risk."

It took Judge Mize 118 days to reach a decision. (By that time, Meredith had also missed the university's fall semester.) The judge said: "The overwhelming weight of the testimony is that . . . [Meredith] was not denied admission because of his color or race." Mize went on to make the absurd claim that the University of Mississippi was not segregated.

Justice had not been served. There was nothing to do but go to a higher court called the United States Court of Appeals for the Fifth Circuit. Meredith knew all along that the battle would be tough. He was one man fighting an entire history of prejudice.

Battle Cry

Meredith missed two more semesters while the court fought over his future. It was a long, tough year of waiting—a year in which Meredith and Motley put up with terrible insults and read biased articles about their case in southern newspapers.

Since the restaurants near the courthouse were for "whites only," even finding lunch was a problem. Perhaps worst of all, day after day, Meredith and Motley sat in the courtroom facing a huge mural of a beautiful southern plantation. In the background was a mansion. In the foreground black slaves picked cotton. Even though slavery had been outlawed for a full century, the state of Mississippi still seemed to mourn its passing.

Finally, on June 25, 1962, the U.S. Fifth Circuit Court overruled Judge Mize's decision: "We find that James Meredith's application for transfer to the University of Mississippi was turned down solely because he was a Negro."

Meredith had won his case! He was ready to enroll when another barrier was put in his way. On July 18, another Federal District judge, Ben Cameron, stated that Meredith could not enroll in the university. It took a ruling by Supreme Court Justice Hugo L. Black on September 10, 1962, to insist that he could.

But no decision made by the Supreme Court was going to change the deeply held belief of many white southerners. Even as Meredith got ready to register for class, Mississippi Governor Ross R. Barnett made a public announcement. He said, in short, that he would never yield on the issue.

"We must either submit to the unlawful dictates of the federal government or stand up like men and tell them *'NEVER!'* " he cried.

The Lines
Are Drawn

When the day finally came for Meredith to enroll, Governor Barnett declared himself the official registrar of the university. Despite what the Court of Appeals and the Supreme Court had ordered, Barnett wanted personally to keep Meredith out of Ole Miss.

Mississippi governor Ross Barnett stood firmly against the integration of Ole Miss.

Feelings ran high among students who supported segregation.

At this point, federal marshals, led by James P. McShane and John Doar, were brought in to protect Meredith. There was good reason to fear that someone would try to kill him.

When Meredith, Motley, Mc-Shane, and Doar drove onto the campus, they were met by swarms of people. Hundreds of state troopers were on hand to keep the crowd, mostly students, under control. Meredith walked through the mob and into the registration building. After a bit of small talk, he said that he would like to register. Governor Barnett replied that things might get violent. Motley protested. She told the governor that she would take action. With those words, Meredith and his crew hustled back to their car. They sped away past a horde of rock-throwing, cursing students.

Round one went to Barnett.

But Meredith was not finished. Robert Kennedy, the attorney general of the United States and younger brother of President John F. Kennedy, called the governor. He insisted that

Meredith have another chance. Barnett agreed to register him at the Mississippi state building instead of at the campus. This time Meredith and the crowd of marshals were met by a mob chanting, ''Nigger, go home!''

Even worse, once inside, Barnett broke his promise to Robert Kennedy and again denied Meredith admission.

But Meredith was determined to try once more. On his third attempt to register, he and federal marshals were met by a mob of state troopers and sheriffs. Governor Barnett was not there. In his place, Lieutenant Governor Paul Johnson blocked the path to the registration building. Marshal McShane demanded that Meredith be allowed to pass. Johnson refused. There was a pushing and shoving match between Johnson, McShane, and other federal marshals and state troopers. Meredith and his supporters retreated for a third time.

Marshal James McShane (center) argued with Lieutenant Governor Paul Johnson (left), who blocked Meredith's entrance to the campus.

ROBERT KENNEDY

Robert Kennedy began to serve his country at a young age. As chief counsel for the Senate committee that investigated improper labor activities in the 1950s, he became a public figure when he uncovered the shady doings of labor leader Jimmy Hoffa.

His brother, President John F. Kennedy, appointed him attorney general in 1961. His key role in the James Meredith crisis put him in the spotlight right away. The other important people behind the desegregation of Ole Miss, President Kennedy and Medgar Evers, were both assassinated in 1963, the year Meredith graduated.

Robert Kennedy continued to serve as attorney general under President Lyndon Johnson. He resigned in 1964 and was elected to the Senate from New York in the fall of that year.

After serving as a senator for three years, he made a bid for the presidency. In June 1968, Robert Kennedy, like his brother John, was killed by an assassin's bullet.

The conflict was getting more and more heated. As Meredith wrote: "It was clearly evident that nothing short of pure force would budge Mississippi from its . . . position."

Attorney General Kennedy ordered fifty federal marshals to accompany Meredith for a fourth try. But as his car was speeding down the road toward the university, an order came over the radio to turn back: The campus was engulfed by a huge mob. As Governor Barnett had said to Robert Kennedy over the phone, "There is liable to be a hundred people killed here . . ."

For the fourth time, James Meredith was turned away.

"I Love Her Customs!"

By Friday, September 28, 1962, truckloads of white racists had arrived on campus to see to it that a black man would never be a student at their school.

It was becoming clear that the federal marshals would not be able to keep the peace. For the first time, President Kennedy called Barnett. The governor, awed by the president, agreed to enroll Meredith the next day.

But that evening, Governor Barnett went to an Ole Miss football game. During halftime, the crowd of some 40,000 people

After talking through most of the night about the Meredith situation, President John F. Kennedy (right) and Attorney General Robert Kennedy continued their discussion in the morning.

began chanting for him to make a speech. Try as he might, Barnett could not hide his true feelings. ''I love Mississippi!'' he cried. ''I love her people, her customs!'' And finally, ''I love and respect her heritage!''

The crowd cheered loud and long. Barnett felt a strong tie to the people of his state. How could he turn his back on hundreds of years of southern traditions? And so he went back on his word to President Kennedy. He decided against enrolling Meredith.

The Kennedys were furious. After some heated phone calls, Governor Barnett finally agreed to a plan: Meredith would enter the school Sunday night. Meanwhile, the governor would be at the state capitol with his followers. Then Barnett would supposedly learn that Meredith had been registered behind his back. He could angrily claim that the Kennedys had tricked him. That way, Mississippians would still believe that he was on their side.

"Tradition
of Honor"

As the sun set that Sunday evening, thousands of racists had gathered in front of the Ole Miss registration building.

"Two-four-six-eight, we ain't gonna integrate!" they chanted.

Worried, Robert Kennedy asked Barnett to assure him that Mississippi state troopers would help the federal marshals keep the peace. Grumbling, Barnett said yes.

In the early evening, President Kennedy addressed the nation on television: "Even among law-abiding men few laws are universally loved, but they are uniformly respected and not resisted. Americans are free, in short, to disagree with the law but not to disobey it."

Kennedy ended by asking the students of Ole Miss to "uphold" a "tradition of honor." In other words, to peacefully accept James Meredith as a fellow student.

But the president was to have no such luck. The crowd was completely out of control. The state troopers Governor Barnett had promised were yet to arrive as the mob moved in on the federal marshals. Bricks, rocks, broken glass, and pieces of concrete benches flew at the marshals.

At this time, unknown to the protesters, Meredith was driven to Baxter Hall, a men's dormitory on another part of the cam-

*On September 30, marshals in riot gear stood
guard at the university. Later that night,
the frenzied crowd erupted into violence.*

pus. While students rioted at the registration building, Meredith walked peacefully to his room, unpacked, read in bed until around ten o'clock, then called it a day. He was probably the only person on campus that night to get a good night's sleep.

The fight at the main campus grew worse. Soon, the federal marshals had no choice but to use tear gas to push back the crowd. But the fumes only made the mob angrier. Many stormed the building. Some tossed bottles filled with gasoline. The air was filled with screams and curses. By dawn two people had been killed, and hundreds of demonstrators and marshals were wounded.

At midnight, Governor Barnett asked for radio time. The Kennedys hoped he would make an appeal for order. Instead, Barnett ended his speech with the words, "We will never surrender!"

President Kennedy was furious. "Listen Governor," he said over the phone, "people have been shot down there already and it's going to get worse. Most of it's happened since those [state] police left and I want them back. Goodbye."

Soon, fifty state troopers returned to help keep order. But it was much too little, far too late. The only real help would come from the army. But they were way behind schedule. Disorganized, it took them over an hour to travel the half mile between the campus and the local airport.

Rioters are arrested on the morning after the bloody battle on campus.

When the troops and the Mississippi National Guard finally arrived, order was restored. At eight o'clock the next morning, Meredith registered.

School at Last

"No student should have to be subjected to the sort of ordeal I had to undergo during the first semester," Meredith wrote later.

Having earned college credits both in the Air Force and at

Jackson, Meredith only needed to take courses for one year at Ole Miss to graduate. During that year at the university, though, Meredith never left his room without the protection of at least one federal marshal. Each day Meredith had to hear ugly racist slurs.

But he made it through to graduation and lived to write, "Perhaps the most remarkable achievement of my three years in Mississippi fighting the system of 'White Supremacy' is that I survived."

On August 18, 1963, Meredith received his diploma, taking comfort that through his actions, perhaps his own son could one day be governor or president. And, in fact, the following year, the first Mississippi schools

Meredith graduated from the University of Mississippi on August 18, 1963.

started to integrate. By 1969, the Supreme Court had ordered all of Mississippi's schools to desegregate. At last, black children and white children went to school together. The tide had begun to turn.

Afterward

After college, Meredith spent a year studying in Nigeria, West Africa. He then went to law school at Columbia University, in New York City. In 1966 he published a book about his experiences called *Three Years in Mississippi*.

In that same year, Meredith began a march from Memphis, Tennessee, to Jackson, Mississippi, to show that black people were free to walk through the land. Within hours of starting out, he was shot and wounded by a sniper's bullet.

Martin Luther King, Jr., and other major civil rights leaders joined together in protest. Arm in arm, they led waves of marchers to complete the James Meredith March Against Fear.

Meredith recovered from his wounds and went on to begin a career as a stockbroker. He also lectured to college students about civil rights and the burning need to address age-old racial strife.

Facing page: James Meredith starts out on the 225-mile March Against Fear from Memphis, Tennessee, to Jackson, Mississippi, in 1966.

IMPORTANT EVENTS IN THE LIFE OF JAMES MEREDITH

1933   James Meredith is born on June 25 in Kosciusko, Mississippi.

1951   Meredith enters the United States Air Force.

1954   *Brown* v. *Board of Education of Topeka* strikes down the policy of "separate but equal" schools.

1960   Meredith returns to Mississippi.

1961   Meredith applies to the University of Mississippi. On August 10, his case is heard by Federal District Judge Sidney Mize, who decides against Meredith.

1962   On June 25, the (Fifth Circuit) U.S. Court of Appeals overrules Judge Mize's decision.
        On September 20, Meredith tries to enroll for the first time.
        On October 1, Meredith is registered at the university.

1963   On August 18, Meredith graduates from the University of Mississippi with a bachelor's degree in political science.

1966   Meredith leads the March Against Fear.

FIND OUT MORE ABOUT
JAMES MEREDITH AND HIS TIMES

The Civil Rights Movement in America from 1865 to the Present by Patricia and Fredrick McKissack (Chicago: Childrens Press, 1987).

John Fitzgerald Kennedy: America's Youngest President by Lucy P. Frisbee (New York: Macmillan, 1986).

Robert Kennedy by Daniel J. Petrillo (New York: Chelsea House, 1989).

Thurgood Marshall: The Fight for Equal Justice by Debra Hess (Englewood Cliffs, N.J.: Silver Burdett Press, 1990).

Thurgood Marshall and Equal Rights by Seamus Cavan (Brookfield, Conn.: The Millbrook Press, 1993).

James Meredith in 1986.

INDEX